The German Oral Examination

*Certificate of
Secondary Educat...
and General Certi...
of Education –
Ordinary Level*

ELSPETH CORRIE

Elspeth Corrie/'84

M

Macmillan Education
London and Basingstoke

First published 1984

Published by
MACMILLAN EDUCATION LIMITED
Houndmills Basingstoke Hampshire RG21 2XS
and London
Associated companies throughout the world

Printed in Hong Kong

British Library Cataloguing in Publication Data

Corrie, Elspeth
   The German oral examination.
   1. German language–Examinations
   2. German language–Study and teaching (Secondary)
   I. Title
   438.3'421'076   PF3068.G7

   ISBN 0-333-36536-4

Foreword

The oral part of German 16+ examinations has gained in importance over the last few years. On average, 30% of your overall mark can come from your oral test, so it is to be taken seriously.

General preparation for the oral test

The best possible preparation is obviously an extended stay in Germany with a German-speaking family. For many pupils, however, this is impossible and, even if you have been on such a visit, lessons can provide you with a lot of valuable practice. Do not assume that only writing is 'work' — work at talking too, and give listening to and speaking German as much concentration as reading and writing it. Take any chance you have to read German aloud and to answer questions. Learn by making mistakes and having them corrected, and by listening to what your teacher and fellow pupils are saying. The more German you hear, the more you will understand and the better your accent and intonation will automatically become.

If your school has a language laboratory take every opportunity to make mistakes in its privacy to a tape which can neither laugh nor shout at you! If you have a radio with FM facility, you should be able to get some German somewhere on that band. Do not expect to understand every word, but just hearing the rise and fall of the language as spoken by a native speaker will improve your oral performance.

Finally, follow the preparation hints that I have given you for each section of the test and take your learning seriously; any learning you do will serve you in your written papers as well.

Examination room technique

Once you have prepared your language as well as you can, you can work on the impression you create in very simple ways.

Sound confident and interested in what you are saying, even if you are not! Speak clearly, do not mumble, and put as much expression into your voice as possible. Look at the examiner while you are talking, not at your feet or out of the window: you do not have to look deep into his eyes (you will make him nervous!), the fly on his left ear will do!

Lastly, there is no point in panic: accept the fact that the examination is now happening to you, will soon be over, and is not the beginning of the end of the world. You may as well keep cool and get on with it to the best of your ability.

Note: I have referred to the examiner throughout as 'he' purely to avoid the cumbersome 'he or she' and 'his or her'.

Acknowledgements

The author is grateful to the following examining bodies for allowing her to use passages from their past papers:

ALSEB: The Associated Lancashire Schools Examining Board for the Certificate of Secondary Education

Cambridge: The University of Cambridge Local Examinations Syndicate

EAEB: The East Anglian Examinations Board for the Certificat of Secondary Education

NWREB: The North West Regional Examinations Board for the Certificate of Secondary Education

YREB: The Yorkshire and Humberside Regional Examinations Board for the Certificate of Secondary Education

Contents

Contents

1 General conversation

Practically every oral examination, whatever the board, involves some general conversation which can range from details of your name and age, through your plans for the future to the culture of Germany. This general conversation time is designed to test your fluency, the spontaneity of your answers, your pronunciation and your grammatical accuracy.

Preparation hints

The best possible preparation for this part of the examination is, of course, a stay in Germany with a non-English speaking family. If you are lucky, you may well have managed to get abroad on some sort of exchange by the time you reach the fifth year. This is not, however, always possible, and often the classroom has to be the place of preparation. There is a list of questions, theme by theme, at the end of this chapter, so before the examination you should have learnt set phrases necessary to answer these and similar questions. For example, learn how to give your address in the German manner – 'Hauptstraße sieben', not 'Nummer sieben Hauptstraße' – and make certain that you have German numbers for your age and your family's ages at your fingertips.

Get as much practice as you can, in class with your teacher or just with your friends, at asking and answering questions. If you are taking the examination for one of the boards which gives you a reading passage to prepare for the oral, be aware that the examiner might use the passage to lead into the general conversation. If, for instance, the passage is about school, he may well open the conversation with questions about your school. So, while you are preparing the reading passage, do not forget to consider its subject as well as how to pronounce the individual words. Incidentally, this will also make you read better!

As you will see from the example questions below, you will need mainly the present tense if you are taking a CSE examination, although a couple of questions will probably demand answers in the past and future. For an 'O' level you will certainly need these three tenses and, if the examiner finds you are coping well with these, he may slip in some questions which involve you in using the pluperfect and conditional too. Since this is an oral exercise, the past tense to be used most is the perfect. You must, therefore, brush up on your tenses so that you can use them accurately. Only with grammatical accuracy as well as fluency will you gain full marks in this section of the examination.

You will also see from the following examples that full sentences are not always necessary in your answers. Firstly, this is meant to be a natural and spontaneous conversation as far as is possible under the circumstances, and secondly, full sentences often waste time without gaining you any extra marks. For example, if you are asked: 'Wie heißt der Direktor dieser Schule?' and you answer: 'Der Direktor dieser Schule heißt Herr Braun', you have wasted the first four or five words – you will gain no marks for a simple correct repetition of the examiner's words and you are wasting time. A more sensible, natural answer would have been: 'Er heißt Herr Braun', or just: 'Herr Braun'; both prove perfectly well that you have understood the question, and such a question demands little more than prompt comprehension and response.

Finally, as part of your preparation, make certain that you have enough 'emergency phrases' at your command to ensure that the conversation is entirely in German; there is a list of these at the end of the chapter.

MODEL CSE TEST

Basic personal information

Q Wie heißen Sie?
A Ich heiße Fred.
Q Wo wohnen Sie?
A Ich wohne Hauptstraße sieben in Brentwood.
Q Wie alt sind Sie?
A Ich bin sechzehn (Jahre alt).

Q Beschreiben Sie mir Ihr Haus!
A Es ist groß; wir haben fünf Schlafzimmer und einen großen, schönen Garten.

Family

Q Haben Sie Geschwister?
A Ja, eine Schwester und einen Bruder.
Q Wie alt ist Ihre Schwester?
A Sie ist neun.
Q Helfen Sie manchmal im Haushalt?
A Ja.
Q Wie?
A Ich räume mein Zimmer auf, ich spüle und ich trockne ab.

School

Q Wann beginnt die Schule morgens?
A Um Viertel nach neun.
Q Was für Fächer haben Sie?
A Deutsch, English, Sport, Erdkunde . . .
Q Welches ist Ihr Lieblingsfach?
A Sport.
Q Warum?
A Ich spiele gern Fußball und ich schwimme sehr gern.

Weather and time

Q Wie ist das Wetter heute?
A Es regnet und der Himmel ist dunkel.
Q Der wievielte ist heute?
A Es ist der vierte Mai.
Q Welche Jahreszeit haben Sie am liebsten?
A Den Sommer.
Q Warum?
A Weil es warm ist, und man kann im Sommer Tennis spielen und schwimmen gehen.

Germany

Q Was essen die Deutschen gewöhnlich zum Abendbrot?
A Sie essen Brot und Wurst und Käse.
Q Wie heißt die Hauptstadt von der BRD?
A Sie heißt Bonn.
Q Wann ist Fasching?
A Fasching ist am Dienstag nach Rosenmontag.

Q Was machen die Deutschen dann?
A Sie haben Karneval und Maskenbälle.

MODEL 'O' LEVEL TEST

Basic personal information

Q Wie ist Ihr Name?
A Mein Name ist/Ich heiße Fred.
Q Wie alt waren Sie letztes Jahr?
A Ich war fünfzehn (Jahre alt).
Q Wie ist Ihre Adresse?
A Meine Adresse ist Hauptstraße sieben, Brentwood.
Q Wo ist Brentwood?
A Brentwood ist sechs Kilometer entfernt.

Family

Q Haben Sie Geschwister?
A Ja, ich habe eine Schwester und einen Bruder.
Q Wer ist das älteste Kind Ihrer Familie?
A Mein Bruder ist der Älteste, er ist achtzehn.
Q In welchem Jahr ist er geboren?
A Er ist neunzehnhundertsechsundsechzig geboren.
Q Was haben Sie heute zum Frühstück gegessen?
A Ich habe Speck, ein Spiegelei, Toast, Butter und Orangenmarmelade gegessen und dazu Kaffee getrunken.

School

Q Wann werden Sie heute nachmittag die Schule verlassen?
A Um Viertel vor vier.
Q Seit wie lange studieren Sie schon Deutsch?
A Ich studiere seit drei Jahren Deutsch.
Q Was möchten Sie machen, wenn Sie die Schule verlassen haben?
A Ich möchte Polizist werden.
Q Was würden Sie heute abend tun, wenn Sie keine Hausaufgaben hätten?
A Ich würde zuerst mit meinen Freunden Fußball spielen und dann fernsehen.

Germany

Q Sind Sie schon mal in Deutschland gewesen?

A Ja, letztes Jahr.

Q Wo waren Sie und wie lange?

A Ich war zwei Wochen lang in Hamburg.

Q Wenn Sie viel Geld hätten, wo würden Sie Ihren Urlaub in Deutschland verbringen?

A In Bayern.

Q Warum?

A Weil die Landschaft sehr schön ist; München ist eine tolle Stadt, und im Winter kann man in den Alpen skifahren.

Vocabulary testers

Q Was machen Sie, wenn Sie Durst haben?

A Ich trinke.

Q Beschreiben Sie mir, was Sie heute tragen!

A Ich trage meine Schuluniform, also ein hellblaues Hemd und eine dunkelblaue Hose mit schwarzen Schuhen, eine dunkelblaue Jacke und eine rotblau gestreifte Krawatte.

Q Was essen Sie am liebsten?

A Pommes Frites oder Eis.

Q Können Sie mir Ihre beste Freundin beschreiben?

A Sie heißt Joanne und ist fünfzehn Jahre alt. Sie hat langes, blondes Haar und blaue Augen. Sie lächelt sehr viel, und in ihrer Freizeit spielt sie Federball oder geht tanzen.

LISTS OF LIKELY QUESTIONS BY TOPIC

Basic personal information

1 Wie heißen Sie?
2 Wie ist Ihr Name/Vorname?
3 Wie alt sind Sie?
4 Wie alt sind Sie am letzten Geburtstag geworden?
5 Wie alt werden Sie am nächsten Geburtstag werden/sein?
6 Wann sind Sie geboren?
7 In welchem Jahre sind Sie geboren?
8 Wann haben Sie Geburtstag?
9 Wo wohnen Sie?
10 Wie ist Ihre Adresse?

Home and family

1 Wohnen Sie in einem Haus oder einer Wohnung?
2 Beschreiben Sie mir Ihr Haus/Ihre Wohnung!
3 Beschreiben Sie mir ein Zimmer Ihres Hauses!
4 Haben Sie Geschwister? Welche?
5 Wie groß ist Ihre Familie?
6 Wer ist das älteste/jüngste Kind?
7 Helfen Sie manchmal bei der Hausarbeit/im Haushalt? Wie?
8 Wenn Sie reich wären, würden Sie ein Haus auf dem Land oder in der Stadt kaufen? Warum?

School

1 Wann fängt die Schule morgens an?
2 Wann sind Sie heute zur Schule gekommen?
3 Wie sind Sie zur Schule gekommen?
4 Wie kommen Sie morgens zur Schule?
5 Wann gehen/fahren Sie nachmittags nach Hause?
6 Wann werden Sie heute nachmittag nach Hause gehen/fahren?
7 Wieviele Schüler gibt es in dieser Schule/in Ihrer Deutschklasse?
8 Welche Fächer haben Sie in der Schule?
9 Welches ist Ihr Lieblingsfach?
10 Seit wie lange studieren Sie schon Deutsch?
11 Seit wie lange sind Sie schon an dieser Schule?
12 Was werden Sie heute abend nach den Hausaufgaben machen?
13 Was würden Sie heute abend machen, wenn Sie keine Hausaufgaben hätten?

Hobbies and future work

1 Was machen Sie am liebsten in Ihrer Freizeit?
2 Haben Sie ein Hobby?
3 Wofür interessieren Sie sich?
4 Was ist Ihre Lieblingsfernsehsendung? Warum?
5 Was für Sportarten treiben Sie am liebsten? Warum?
6 Was ist Ihr Lieblingssport? Warum?
7 Wann werden Sie die Schule verlassen?
8 Was möchten Sie werden, wenn Sie die Schule verlassen (haben)?
9 Wo möchten Sie arbeiten?

German background studies

1 Sind Sie schon mal in Deutschland gewesen? Wann? Wo?

2   Möchten Sie mal Deutschland besuchen? Welchen Teil?

3   Beschreiben Sie mir eine Stadt Deutschlands, die Sie kennen!

4   Was ißt man gewöhnlich zum Frühstück/zum Abendbrot in Deutschland?

5   In welchem Lande der Bundesrepublik kann man skifahren?

6   Welchen Teil Deutschlands möchten Sie am liebsten besuchen? Warum?

7   Wie heißt der Bundeskanzler?

8   Was ist Karneval?

9   Nennen Sie vier Länder, die Mitglieder der EG sind!

10 Was ist die Hauptstadt der DDR/BRD?

11 Wann beginnt eine deutsche Schule morgens?

12 In welchen Ländern spricht man Deutsch?

13 Welche Länder grenzen an Deutschland im Süden?

14 Was für eine Stadt ist Hamburg?

15 Wie heißt das Geld in Österreich/der Schweiz?

Weather, time and seasons

1   Wie ist das Wetter heute?

2   Wie war das Wetter gestern?

3   Welche Jahreszeit haben Sie am liebsten? Warum?

4   In welchem Monat haben Sie Geburtstag?

5   Der wievielte ist heute?

6   Den wievielten haben wir heute?

7   Wie spät ist es?

8   Um wieviel Uhr gehen Sie gewöhnlich ins Bett/kommen Sie zur Schule/fahren Sie nach Hause/stehen Sie gewöhnlich auf?

9   Wann werden Sie heute ins Bett gehen?

10 Wann sind Sie heute aufgestanden?

Shopping, dress and animals

1   Beschreiben Sie, was Sie heute tragen/ich heute trage!

2   Was ziehen Sie an, wenn Sie abends mit Freunden ausgehen?

3   Wo kann man Gemüse/Brot/Fleisch/Bücher/Zeitungen kaufen?

4   Was verkauft ein Metzger/ein Bäcker/ein Wirt?

5   Mögen Sie Haustiere? Welche? Warum?

6   Haben Sie Haustiere? Was für welche?

Vocabulary testers

1   Was machen Sie, wenn Sie müde/durstig/hungrig sind?

2   Was machen Sie, wenn Sie Durst/Hunger haben?

3   Wann machen Sie Ihre schriftliche Prüfung in Deutsch?

4   Glauben Sie, Sie werden sie bestehen?

5   Warum geht man zu einer Bücherei/einem Friseur/einer Wäscherei/einem Arzt/einem Zahnarzt?

Emergency phrases

These can come in useful if you do not understand a question or if you simply want time to think!

Wie bitte?
Entschuldigung, ich habe die Frage nicht verstanden!
Würden Sie bitte die Frage wiederholen?
Das habe ich nicht verstanden!

2 Role-playing and situational dialogues

The role-playing or situational dialogue test is common to both CSE and GCE 'O' level examinations and is very likely to form part of the oral testing in the 16+ examinations. This element is designed to test areas of functional language, in other words it is your chance to show your ability to survive in Germany in various practical, everyday situations. This is your chance to prove that you can communicate a set of specific messages clearly.

Preparation hints

Before your oral examination you should revise vocabulary relevant to the various topics commonly covered by this test. There is a list of such topics at the end of this chapter.

Once you have been given your role-play cards at the start of your examination you will be given some preparation time. Read through the situation as outlined on the card carefully and make sure that you know what basic points of information you have to communicate. Once you have done this it is best to forget the actual English words entirely. There is no point at all in trying to translate. Think yourself into the situation in German and try to imagine yourself in that exact position in Germany. If you do not know a particular set phrase which seems vital (e.g. 'einmal nach Köln, bitte, hin und zurück'), do not panic! Work out how you could get the same message across using words that you do know ('eine Karte nach Köln, bitte. Ich fahre auch zurück.'). Of course it is best if you have all the right phrases at your fingertips, but keep in mind that what you are really trying to do is make a German person understand what you want rather than impress them with your perfect German. On this same theme, it is far better to use simple language which is clear than to try to be very complicated and fail to communicate your message. Finally, be aware of your relationship to your dialogue partner: use 'Sie' if you are supposed to be talking to a stranger or being formal and polite, but, of course, 'du' must be used if you are talking to a friend or child.

Practise your part of the dialogue as much as you can before you are called into the examination room. Remember that the more little 'extras' you can slip into the conversation once you begin, the better. There is a list of such extras at the end of this chapter including a section on ways of hesitating in German! The main thing to remember whilst you are actually in the examination room is that this is a dialogue and not a monologue. Do listen to what the examiner says and react in some way. He may well slip in some awkward supplementary question (of which there are some examples at the end of the chapter) and, apart from anything else, his replies or questions may very well give you clues of vocabulary or grammar to help you with your next contribution to the dialogue. So, carry out a conversation, do not just sit glassy-eyed in front of the examiner chanting your part at him and ignoring what he says!

MODEL DIALOGUES

Role-play card 1

You are in a Gasthaus with a friend. The examiner is the waiter.

(a) Ask if there is a table free.
(b) Order an ice cream and a coffee.
(c) Say that your friend would like a piece of cake and a lemonade.
(d) Ask for a small spoon.
(e) Ask for the bill.

Examiner: Guten Tag, junger Mann/Fräulein. Sie wünschen?
Candidate: Guten Tag. Haben Sie einen freien Tisch, bitte?
Examiner: Ja, gerne: setzen Sie sich hierhin. Was möchten Sie?
Candidate: Ein Eis und einen Kaffee, bitte.
Examiner: Einmal Eis, einmal Kaffee. Und Ihr Freund?
Candidate: Mein Freund möchte gern ein Stück Kuchen und eine Limonade, bitte.

Examiner: Gerne . . . Bitte schön, die Herrschaften; ist alles in Ordnung?
Candidate: Ich hätte gern einen kleinen Löffel, bitte.
Examiner: Ach ja, Entschuldigung. Hier bitte.
Candidate: Danke sehr. Darf ich bitte zahlen?
Examiner: Bitte schön, Ihre Rechnung.
Candidate: Danke schön, auf Wiedersehen!

Role-play card 2

You telephone a friend but he/she is not at home. The examiner will play the part of your friend's father or mother:
(a) Say hello, give your name and ask if you could speak to Johann/Birgit.
(b) Ask if the mother/father knows when he/she will be back.
(c) Say you wanted to know if he/she could come to the cinema with you tomorrow evening.
(d) Ask if Johann/Birgit could telephone you later this evening.
(e) Say thank you and goodbye.

Examiner: Nul-zwo-sechs-fünf-ein-sechs. Hier Schmidt.
Candidate: Guten Abend, Herr/Frau Schmidt. Alan/Christine am Apparat. Könnte ich bitte mit Johann/Birgit sprechen?
Examiner: Ach, guten Abend, Alan/Christine! Es tut mir leid, aber Johann/Birgit ist nicht zu Hause.
Candidate: Schade! Wissen Sie vielleicht, wann er/sie zurück sein wird?
Examiner: Nun, leider nicht, ich weiß es nicht genau. Kann ich ihm/ihr eine Nachricht von dir geben?
Candidate: Ja, bitte: ich wollte wissen, ob er/sie morgen abend mit mir ins Kino kommen könnte.
Examiner: Na, fein! Soll er/sie dich später anrufen?
Candidate: Ja bitte, es wäre schön, wenn er/sie mich heute abend zurückrufen könnte.
Examiner: Das sag ich ihm/ihr dann. Tschüß, Alan/Christine.
Candidate: Danke, Herr/Frau Schmidt. Auf Wiederhören!

Role-play card 3

You are in a greengrocer's shop. The examiner is the grocer:
(a) Ask if he has any red apples.
(b) Ask for a pound of them, and ask if he has any milk.
(c) Ask for two litres.
(d) Say that is all you want and ask how much you owe.

Examiner: Guten Tag, kann ich Ihnen behilflich sein?
Candidate: Guten Tag. Haben Sie rote Äpfel?
Examiner: Ja, rote Äpfel habe ich; sie kosten DM 4 das Kilo.
Candidate: Gut, ich nehme also ein Pfund, bitte. Haben Sie auch Milch?
Examiner: Ja, wieviel möchten Sie denn?
Candidate: Zwei Liter, bitte.
Examiner: Zwei Liter Milch. Sonst noch was?
Candidate: Das wär's danke. Wieviel kostet das also?
Examiner: Zehn Mark bitte, mein Herr/meine Dame.
Candidate: Bitte schön.
Examiner: Vielen Dank. Auf Wiedersehen!
Candidate: Auf Wiedersehen!

Here are some examples of role-play cards for you to practise on.

Role-play card 4

You are staying with a German friend. The examiner is your friend's mother/father and is giving you breakfast.
(a) Say you have slept well and would like coffee with milk.
(b) Tell him/her that you would like to go into town today to buy some postcards.
(c) Say that you would like to go with him/her and ask when the bus leaves.
(d) Say that you will be ready in ten minutes.

Vocabulary

schlafen   to sleep

ich möchte I would like
Ansichtskarten postcards
um . . . zu (+ infinitive) in order to . . .
mitkommen to come/go with
abfahren, fährt . . . ab to depart, departs
in zehn Minuten in ten minutes
fertig ready

Role-play card 5

You are at a garage in Germany. The examiner is the attendant.
(a) Ask for 20 litres of petrol.
(b) Say you do not want anything else, but ask the way to Steinkirche.
(c) Ask how far it is.
(d) Pay the attendant, say thank you and goodbye.

Vocabulary

zwanzig Liter Super 20 litres of 4 star
das wäre alles that is all
wie komme ich am besten nach . . . ? how do I get to . . . ?
weit far

Role-play card 6

You are talking to a German friend about your interests. The examiner will play the part of your friend.
(a) Tell your friend you like tennis and swimming and ask if he/she likes sport.
(b) Ask if there is a sports club in his/her town.
(c) Say that you also like to listen to music.
(d) Tell him/her what sort of music you like best and ask if he/she has many records.

Vocabulary

ich . . . gern I like . . .
der Sportverein sports club

am liebsten best of all
die Schallplatte record

Role-play card 7

You are in your home town, and a stranger comes up to you who speaks only German. Your examiner is the stranger.
(a) Tell him/her that you can speak German.
(b) Direct him to the railway station — first left, third right and then straight ahead.
(c) Say that it is quite a long way and it is best to go by bus.
(d) Say that you are going to the bus station and will go with the stranger.

Vocabulary

ich spreche . . . I can speak . . .
der Bahnhof station
erste first
dritte third
geradeaus straight ahead
ziemlich weit quite far
am besten best
mit dem Bus by bus
der Busbahnhof bus station

Role-play card 8

You are on a long-distance train travelling from Ostend to Vienna. The examiner is the Passport Control Officer who boards the train at the German frontier.
(a) Say here is your ticket.
(b) Apologize and say that you did not understand.
(c) Say that you are travelling to Austria.
(d) Ask what time the train arrives in Cologne.
(e) Say thank you.

(EAEB, CSE)

die Fahrkarte   ticket
verstehen   to understand
fahren   to travel
nach (+ name of place or country)   to
Österreich   Austria
ankommen   to arrive
Köln   Cologne

Role-play card 9

You are buying tickets for a concert. The examiner will play the part of the box-office clerk.
(a) Ask for two tickets for Thursday.
(b) Ask how much the tickets cost.
(c) Say you will take two tickets at 8 DM.
(d) Ask when the concert finishes
(e) Say thank you and goodbye.

(EAEB, CSE)

Vocabulary

die Karte   ticket
zu acht Mark   at 8 Marks
zu Ende sein   to finish
das Konzert   concert

Role-play card 10

You are at a German bank to change some English money into German money. The examiner will play the part of the bank clerk.
(a) Say you want to change £20 into German money.
(b) Ask how many marks there are to the £ today.
(c) Ask if he needs your passport.
(d) Say you would like 10-mark notes.
(e) Say thank you and goodbye.

(EAEB, CSE)

Vocabulary

wechseln   to change (money)
Pfund   pounds sterling
pro Pfund   to the pound
der 10 Mark Schein   ten Mark note

Role-play card 11

You have lost your wallet in a German town and you have gone to the Police Station to report your loss. The examiner is the officer behind the desk.
(a) Say that you have lost your wallet.
(b) Say that it is brown and has your name and address in it.
(c) Say it had a 20-Mark note and some stamps in it.

(EAEB, CSE)

Vocabulary

die Brieftasche   wallet
verlieren   to lose
darin   in it
der 20 Mark Schein   20 Mark note
einige   some
die Briefmarke   stamp

Role-play card 12

You are staying with a German family and have hurt your leg. The doctor arrives to see you. The examiner is the doctor.
(a) Say that your right leg hurts.
(b) Say that you fell over in the street.
(c) Ask how long you will have to stay indoors.

(EAEB, CSE)

Vocabulary

das Bein   leg
recht   right

weh tun   to hurt
fallen   to fall
auf der Straße   in the street
zu Hause   at home
bleiben   to stay

Role-play card 13

You are in a post-office in Germany. The examiner is the counter-clerk.
(a) Say you want to send a parcel to England.
(b) Ask when the parcel is likely to arrive.
(c) Ask how much a letter to England costs.

(EAEB, CSE)

Vocabulary

das Paket   parcel
schicken   to send
ankommen   to arrive
der Brief   letter

Role-play card 14

You are staying in München and because there is an air-traffic controllers strike you have to travel home by train and boat. You go to the travel agency.
(a) Explain that you wish to travel home by train and boat.
(b) Ask about times of trains to Ostende via Köln.
(c) Ask how long the boat journey from Ostende to Dover lasts.
(d) Ask if there is a restaurant car on the train.
(e) Ask the price of a single second class train ticket.

(ALSEB, CSE)

Vocabulary

mit dem Zug   by train
mit dem Schiff   by boat

---

wegen des Streiks   because of the strike
über Köln   via Köln
dauern, wie lange dauert . . . ?   to last, how long does . . . last/take?
die Überfahrt   sea crossing
der Speisewagen   restaurant car
eine Einzelkarte   single ticket
zweiter Klasse   second class

Role-play card 15

While staying in Germany you have visited Hannover and have lost your bearings in the town. You address a passer-by.
(a) Tell the person that you do not know Hannover.
(b) Ask the way to the main station.
(c) Ask how far it is to walk and whether there is a bus.
(d) Explain that your train departs at 5 o'clock and ask what the time is now.
(e) Ask the person if there are other trains to Bremen.

(ALSEB, CSE)

Vocabulary

kennen   to know
der Hauptbahnhof   main railway station
der Bus   bus
andere   other

Role-playing card 16

You are travelling by car in Germany and decide to spend a few days in a country area. You go to an hotel for accommodation.
(a) Ask the hotel keeper if there are two rooms available.
(b) Ask the price, with breakfast and evening meal.
(c) Ask advice about walks in the district.
(d) Ask where you can leave the car.
(e) Explain that your grandmother, who is with you, will not be going out walking and would like a midday meal.

(ALSEB, CSE)

Vocabulary

verbringen   to spend (time)
das Zimmer   room
frei   vacant
das Frühstück   breakfast
das Abendessen   evening meal
der Spaziergang   walk
in der Gegend   in the area
lassen   to leave
das Auto/der Wagen   car
die Großmutter   grandmother
spazierengehen   to go for a walk
das Mittagessen   midday meal

Role-play card 17

It is a wet day in Bonn. You decide to visit the Beethovenhaus and the Bundeshaus in the morning and to go to the cinema in the afternoon. You go to the tourist office.
(a) Ask when the first two places are open.
(b) Ask if there is any charge at the Beethovenhaus.
(c) Ask if there are conducted tours of the Bundeshaus.
(d) Ask where these places are.
(e) Ask what films are on and the times of showing.

(ALSEB, CSE)

Vocabulary

aufmachen   to be open
das Beethoven-/Bundeshaus   the Beethoven/Bundeshaus
die Eintrittsgebühr   entrance fee
bezahlen   to pay
der Führer   guide
sich befinden   to be situated
laufen   to run, to be on (film)
der Film, die Filme   film(s)
die Vorführung   showing
beginnen   to start

Role-play card 18

Your car has been broken into while parked overnight outside an hotel in Germany. You speak to a police officer the next morning.
(a) Explain where the car was parked.
(b) Say during what period it was there.
(c) Describe what is missing from the car.
(d) Say that you locked the car, but it was open when you arrived this morning.
(e) Explain that you are travelling on to München, where you will be staying at the 'Bahnhotel'.

(ALSEB, CSE)

Vocabulary

vor einem Hotel   in front of a hotel
war ... geparkt   was parked
über Nacht   overnight
... ist weg   ... has gone
... ist gestohlen worden   ... has been stolen
abschließen   to lock
auf   open
heute morgen   this morning
ankommen   to arrive
weiterfahren   to travel on
das Bahnhotel   the Bahnhotel
sich aufhalten   to stay

Warning   The examiner may not just sit and meekly follow the dialogue outline on the card: it is quite possible, especially in an 'O' level examination, that he will slip in a supplementary question or two. While you are preparing your dialogue, try to anticipate and prepare for possible extra questions. The following examples should give you an idea of what to expect.

Role-play card 19

You are looking for a summer job and have heard that a farmer, the examiner, might have one for you.
(a) Explain why you have come to see him.

(b) Ask what sort of work it is.
(c) Ask when you could begin.
(d) Ask where it is possible to stay locally.

After point (b), the examiner may not immediately offer you the job so that you can go straight on to point (c). He may ask where you come from, why you want to work in this area, whether you have any previous experience of farm work, how long you could work for, and so on.

Role-play card 20

You are at the railway station information office. The examiner is the official.
(a) Ask if there is a train to Hannover tomorrow morning.
(b) Ask if it is an express.
(c) Ask if you can reserve a seat on it.

You may be told after your first question that there are two suitable trains between which you must choose. When you ask to reserve a seat, the examiner may prolong the dialogue by asking for exact details — for example, whether you want a window seat, non-smoker etc.

The main lessons to be deduced from this are, firstly, not to be horrified if the guidelines given on the card are not absolutely rigidly followed, and secondly, to listen carefully to what the examiner says and be prepared to answer him, rather than just ploughing on with your prepared part.

Common role-play topics

Accommodation — booking hotel rooms, registering at youth hostels.
Communications — telephoning, buying stamps.
Directions — asking for and giving them.
Entertainment — buying cinema/theatre tickets, eating and drinking out, going to football matches, etc.
Illness — getting medical treatment, explaining what is wrong.
Losing/finding something — reporting it to the authorities.

Shopping — asking prices, buying/rejecting articles.
Staying away from home — at a hotel, youth hostel, campsite, pen-friend's house; finding out about the routine and where things are.
Travel — abroad: going through customs and immigration, changing money.
Travel by car: buying petrol, having a breakdown, having an accident.
Travel by public transport: asking for tickets, about fares, about departure and arrival times, types of train, etc.

You would be sensible to go through this list learning the constructions (wie komme ich am besten zum/zur/nach . . . ?) and specialised vocabulary ('auf Wiederhören', 'Geld wechseln') which are almost bound to come up in dealing with each topic. Obviously you cannot be sure that it will be a pair of shoes you are asked to buy, for example, but if you have learnt phrases like 'Größe 38' and 'darf ich . . . anprobieren?' you can face any shopping topic with confidence.

You will earn yourself extra marks in role-playing by giving fairly prompt answers and by including various little extras. Learn a selection of the phrases below and, using them *where appropriate*, you will not fail to impress!

Greetings

Formal:
Guten Tag, Herr/Frau . . .
Auf Wiedersehen!
Auf Wiederhören!
Informal:
Hallo!
Tschüß!

Expressing agreement/acceptance

Ja, klar	Natürlich
Ja, ist gut	Ja, gerne
Genau!	Da hast du/haben Sie recht
(Das) stimmt ja	Das meine ich ja auch
Einverstanden!	Gut! abgemacht!

Expressing pleasure/satisfaction/relief

Na prima!	Wunderschön!

Gott sei Dank! Wunderbar!
Na schön! Toll!

Also nein!
Nein! das glaub(e) ich doch nicht!

Expressing disagreement/refusal

Nein, das sehe ich nicht ein.
Das geht aber nicht!
Das gibt's doch nicht.
Quatsch!
(Das) stimmt nicht!

Expressing thanks

Danke (schön/sehr).
Vielen Dank.
Recht herzlichen Dank.
Ich danke Ihnen/dir.
Ich bedanke mich sehr.

Expressing annoyance/displeasure/indignation

Also nein!
Um Gotteswillen!
Das darf doch wohl nicht wahr sein!
Ach nein!
Du meine Güte!
Was *soll* das denn?

Acknowledging thanks

Bitte schön.
Bitte bitte.
Nichts zu danken.

Expressing regret/worry/despair

Entschuldigen Sie bitte.
Ach, Entschuldigung!
Das tut mir aber leid.
Ich mache mir wirklich Sorgen darum.
Was mache ich denn jetzt?

How to hesitate in German

Na ja . . .
Also . . .
Na, mal sehen . . .
Nun . . .
Nun, ganz sicher bin ich nicht, aber . . .
Das genaue Wort fällt mir im Moment nicht ein, aber . . .

Expressing surprise

Ach nein, wirklich?

If you need a repetition

Wie bitte?
Bitte?
Entschuldigung, das hab(e) ich nicht verstanden.

3 The single picture

In almost every CSE, GCE 'O' level and, probably, 16+ examination you will be asked to talk about a picture. Some boards distribute a set of pictures with sets of questions on each in time for you to prepare this element of the oral in class; others ask you to answer questions on and talk about a picture which you have not seen before. These pictures are not designed as vocabulary tests; rather they are there to test your ability to manipulate the German language in describing something.

Preparation hints

Although this is not a lexical test, you do, of course, need to know plenty of vocabulary. The pictures deal with a selection of ordinary, everyday topics, a list of which is at the end of this chapter. You should make sure that you know basic vocabulary for these topics, such as the names of shops, furniture and household vocabulary etc. A perennial complaint of the examination boards is that candidates lack very many basic items of vocabulary; make sure that the same cannot be said of you!

You will also need to be confident in your use of prepositions with the correct cases and be able to describe where people are, what they are going into, coming out of, sitting down on, already sitting on etc. Verbs will be tested, not only in the present tense: you must be able to form the past and future as well in order to answer questions about what people have just done or are just about to do.

Once you are in the examination room, look carefully at the picture if you have not seen it before and listen hard to the examiner – things which are not easy to do if you are nervous. The examiner's questions will give you vocabulary help and tell you which tense to use in your answers. If you need a repetition of a question, say so, but say so in German! Finally,

you do not necessarily need to answer questions in full sentences, but do remember that monosyllables do not impress: answer as fully as possible without getting yourself into deep water with complicated and too detailed answers with which your German cannot cope.

MODEL TESTS

Samstag Nachmittag

Q 1 Wo befinden sich diese Leute?
A 1 (Sie befinden sich) im Wohnzimmer.
Q 2 Wie ist das Wetter?
A 2 Es ist schlechtes Wetter – es donnert und blitzt und regnet, und der Himmel ist dunkel.
Q 3 Was machen die Kinder?
A 3 Sie sitzen auf dem Boden und spielen Karten. Sie trinken dabei Kaffee und essen Kekse.
Q 4 Was hat ihr Vater gelesen?
A 4 Er hat eine Zeitung gelesen.
Q 5 Und was macht er jetzt?
A 5 Jetzt schläft er (im Sessel).
Q 6 Wo sitzt die Katze?
A 6 (Sie sitzt) am Fenster auf dem Fensterbank.
Q 7 Wo ist die Blumenvase?
A 7 (Sie ist) auf dem Bücherregal.
Q 8 Wer hat ein Bier getrunken?
A 8 Der Vater hat es getrunken.
Q 9 Wie spät ist es?
A 9 (Es ist) halb fünf.
Q 10 Was sehen Sie rechts im Hintergrund?
A 10 (Ich sehe) einen Fernsehapparat, ein Film ist im Fernsehen. Ich sehe auch Bücher auf einem Bücherregal, einen Papierkorb und einen Plattenspieler mit zwei Lautsprechern. Unten im Bücherregal sind viele Schallplatten, und eine Blumenvase steht oben darauf.

In der Stadt

Q 1 Wo findet diese Szene statt?
A 1 (Diese Szene findet) auf der Straße in der Stadt (statt).
Q 2 Welche Jahreszeit ist es?
A 2 Es ist Winter.
Q 3 Woher wissen Sie das?
A 3 (Ich weiß das vom Wetter her), es schneit.
Q 4 Was will die Dame im Vordergrund machen?
A 4 Sie will über die Straße gehen.
Q 5 Was hat diese Dame gekauft?
A 5 Sie hat wahrscheinlich Lebensmittel gekauft.
Q 6 Was machen die Mutter und das Kind?

A 6 Sie sehen sich die Bücher im schaufenster an.
Q 7 Was hat der Mann mit dem Hund gerade gemacht?
A 7 Er hat gerade eine Zeitung (beim Zeitungshändler) gekauft.
Q 8 Was hat er an?
A 8 Er trägt einen gestreiften Schal, eine dunkle Jacke, eine Hose und Gummistiefeln.
Q 9 Wie fährt der Junge auf der Straße?
A 9 Er fährt mit dem Rad.
Q 10 Was kann man im Laden links kaufen?
A 10 Da kann man Kleidungsstücke kaufen.

15

Am Bahnhof

Questions

1 Wann fährt der Zug nach Hamburg ab?
2 Was macht der Mann auf der Bank?
3 Wohin geht die Familie im Hintergrund?
4 Was will die Frau am Schalter kaufen?
5 Was kann man sonst am Bahnhof kaufen?
6 Was hat der junge Mann gerade gekauft?
7 Wie spät ist es?
8 Wie lange müssen die zwei jungen Leute auf den Zug nach Kopenhagen warten?
9 Was für Gepäck haben sie?
10 Von welchem Gleis fährt der Zug nach Lübeck?

Vocabulary

um . . . Uhr at . . . o'clock
warten auf (+ accusative) to wait for
das Gleis platform
die Fahrkarte ticket
die Zeitung newspaper
der Koffer suitcase
der Rucksack rucksack

Auf dem Lande

Questions

1 Wo sind wir im Bild?
2 In welchem Land sind wir?
3 Beschreiben Sie die Familie, die im Vordergrund sitzt!
4 Wo genau liegt das Haus?
5 Was macht der Mann mit dem Rucksack?
6 Was für Tiere sehen Sie im Bild?
7 Wo sitzt der Mann mit der Angelrute?
8 Was macht er?
9 Was tragen die Kühe um den Hals?

10 Was kann man in den Bergen machen?

Vocabulary

die Gebirge mountains	**die Schweiz** Switzerland
das Picknick picnic	**das Baby** baby
bestehen aus (+ dative)	to consist of
der Wald wood	**wandern** to hike
die Kuh cow	**am Fluß** by the river
angeln to fish	**die Glocke** bell
skifahren to ski	**klettern** to climb

$$x + y \cdot (3x - ab) : 12$$

In der Schule

Questions

1 Wo findet diese Szene statt?
2 In welcher Unterrichtstunde sind wir?
3 Woher wissen Sie das?
4 Wie ist das Wetter?
5 Warum sieht der Junge zum Fenster hinaus?
6 Wieviele Schüler sind im Klassenzimmer?
7 Warum hat die Schülerin die Hand gehoben?
8 Was sehen Sie an der Wand?

9 Was spielen die Schüler im Vordergrund?
10 Was macht der Schüler links im Vordergrund?

Vocabulary

das Klassenzimmer classroom
die (Unterrichts) Stunde lesson
die Rechenaufgabe sum
die Tafel blackboard   **schreiben** to write
der Lehrer teacher   **sich langweilen** to be bored
eine Frage beantworten to answer a question
eine Frage stellen to ask a question

18

Im Geschäft

Vocabulary

der Verkäufer/die Verkäuferin shop assistant
der Kunde/die Kundin customer
die Kasse cash desk
bezahlen to pay

anprobieren to try on
aussuchen to look out/choose
der Spiegel mirror
das Kleid dress
der Rock skirt
die Einkaufstasche shopping bag

Im Garten

Vocabulary

der Garten garden
die Katze cat
der Vogel bird
fangen to catch
der Baum tree

der Hund dog
der Liegestuhl deckchair
sich ausruhen to rest
der Rasen lawn
mähen to mow
die Blumen flowers
pflücken to pick

Im Gasthaus

Vocabulary

der Kellner/die Kellnerin   waiter/waitress
am Tisch   at the table
die Rechnung   bill
'Zahlen bitte!'   'bill please!'

bestellen   to order
die Uhr   clock
die Speisekarte   menu
an der Wand   on the wall
die Kerzen   candle
ein Bier   beer

Warning As you will have gathered from these examples, questions may well involve you in interpreting the picture, not just reporting the obvious. If you are asked why, for example, someone is going into a particular shop you will have to invent a suitable answer — it will not be sensible to say: 'Um eine Jacke zu kaufen,' if the shop window in the picture is full of motorbikes. Similarly, if asked what the figure who is leaving the pet shop has just done, you will be expected to have noticed that he is carrying a bird in a cage.

The lesson to learn from this is that you must look carefully at the detail of the picture and be psychologically prepared for both the straightforward and less straightforward.

Common picture subjects

Countryside
At home — inside the house
              in the garden
Hotel
Restaurant
Seaside
School
Town — in the street
              inside a shop
Travel — at an airport
              at a harbour
              at a railway station

The pictures will not test any really extraordinary vocabulary, so you can prepare yourself well by learning items which commonly occur when you are dealing with these topics, which, moreover, are very similar to those of the role-play tests and picture essays.

Useful words and phrases for talking about a picture

der Vordergrund; im Vordergrund (in) the foreground
der Hintergrund; im Hintergrund (in) the background
links/rechts im Bild in the left/right of the picture
mitten im Bild/in der Mitte des Bildes in the middle of the
    picture

4 The picture sequence

This test is to be found in both GCE 'O' level and CSE examinations and will probably form part of the 16+ examination. Some boards treat the sequence of pictures in much the same way as the single picture, providing set questions on individual frames. There is not usually any preparation time provided for in this sort of test, but the questions are fairly simple and straightforward. Other boards make the picture sequence a more demanding exercise, giving you a short time before the examination to prepare an oral narrative based on the story. The time you are supposed to talk for varies between two and four minutes. Despite this strict time limit, you are not being tested on how fast you can talk German! The picture sequence tests your ability to present a connected narrative in the past tense.

Preparation

Since the preparation for a picture sequence which has specific questions is necessarily much the same as that for the single picture, this section will concentrate on preparation of an oral narrative. This test is very similar to the picture essay demanded by many written papers, both CSE and 'O' level, so any revision you do for this will serve a useful double purpose.

The first thing to check is obviously the formation of the past tenses: although this is to be spoken, you must use the imperfect tense as it is a story; so, learn common strong or irregular imperfects carefully. The picture sequence also offers you a superb opportunity to show how well you can link the frames of the story with more than just a monotonous 'dann . . . und dann . . .'. There is a list of causal and temporal links, with examples of how to use them, at the end of this chapter. It is by no means exhaustive and you should add to it from your own knowledge.

In the preparation time you are given just before the examination you must look at the picture sequence carefully and work out the basic outline of the story. Make up and repeat to yourself a couple of sentences about each picture and then go back to the beginning and go through it again, this time linking the frames properly. You will need to talk for between two and four minutes. You should ideally have had plenty of practice in class during the run-up to the examination, but remember: this may sound a short time, but it can seem dreadfully long if you have not enough to say!

The examiner may well have some particular story in mind based on the picture sequence, but he is not testing your powers of interpretation, so sound confident in the examination room, even if you find the pictures unclear. Make sure that you produce a sensible and logical narrative and tell it convincingly. Try to put some expression into your voice, despite your nerves. Obviously you will not be given marks purely for your acting ability, but if you tell the story interestingly and interestedly any mistakes will not be as sorely noticeable as in a nervously hesitant or monotonous narration. Remember who you are telling the story to, and look at him or her; if you need to, point at the pictures.

In other words, the main advice is this: do not sit petrified! You may well find it easier to be interested and overcome your nerves if you make yourself the main character in the story and tell it in the first person — this is perfectly permissible.

MODEL PICTURE NARRATIVES

Ein Abend zu Hause

Examiner: Erzählen Sie nun bitte die Geschichte, die Sie vorbereitet haben.

Candidate: Diese Geschichte handelt von einem Mädchen, Sabine. Letzten Montag blieb sie den ganzen Abend zu Hause.

Frame 1: Um sieben Uhr spülte Sabine nach dem Abendessen ab. Sie winkte ihren Eltern zu, die zusammen ins Theater gingen. Sabine war nun allein im Hause.

Frame 2: Nachdem sie abgespült hatte, ging Sabine nach oben in ihr Schlafzimmer, um ihre Hausaufgaben zu machen. Sie hörte dabei ihrer Lieblingsschallplatte zu, weil ihre Hausaufgaben langweilig waren.

Frame 3: Sabine ging um zehn Uhr ins Bett. Draußen regnete es in Strömen und es blitzte, aber sie schlief bald ein.

Frame 4: Plötzlich wurde Sabine aber wach! Es war halb zwölf, und irgendein Geräusch unten hatte sie geweckt. Nun hatte Sabine Angst — war ein Einbrecher vielleicht unten eingebrochen?

Frame 5: Sabine konnte nicht wieder einschlafen, also stand sie mutig auf, nahm eine große Taschenlampe von ihrem Nachttisch und ging leise nach unten.

Frame 6: Als Sabine in die Küche kam, lachte sie laut. Es war kein Einbrecher gewesen, sondern nur ihre kleine Katze. Die Katze hatte versucht, die Milch aus dem Krug zu trinken und hatte dabei den Krug umgekippt. Der Krug war kaputt gegangen — das war das Geräusch, das Sabine geweckt hatte. Nun saß die kleine Katze ruhig auf dem Boden und leckte die Milch auf. Sabine war so erleichtert, daß sie die Katze überhaupt nicht ausschimpfen konnte!

Now you try to make up some narratives about the following sets of pictures. For the first few there are some guiding questions and phrases to help you; the last ones only have vocabulary help.

Frame 1: Wie hießen die drei Männer?
Wo waren sie? Was planten sie?
Was sehen Sie in der Ecke des Zimmers?

der Sparkassenüberfall bank raid
das Gewehr gun

Frame 2: Wo haben die Einbrecher geparkt?
Warum blieb einer im Auto?
Wohin liefen die zwei anderen?
Wer war gerade dabei, mit seinem Hund spazieren-
zugehen?
Was sah er, und was sagte er sich?

vor der/in die Sparkasse in front of/into the bank
der Fahrer driver **die Einbrecher** robbers

Frame 3: Was riefen die Einbrecher?
Was machten die Kassiererinnen?
Was mußte der Sparkassenleiter machen?

Hände hoch! hands up!
schreien to scream **holen** to fetch

Frame 4: Wo war der Junge inzwischen?
Wen rief er an?
Was sagte der Polizist?

die Telefonzelle phone box
anrufen, rief . . . an to phone, phoned
die Polizei the police **der Polizist** policeman
inzwischen meanwhile **gleich** immediately

Frame 5: Wann ist die Polizei angekommen?
Wer war noch in der Bank?
Was machte die Polizei?
Wohin fuhren die Polizisten mit den Einbrechern?

. . . Minuten später . . . minutes later
verhaften to arrest **bringen, brachte** to take,
took
die Polizeiwache police station

Frame 6: Was passierte am folgenden Tag?
Was bekam der Junge vom Sparkassenleiter? Warum?

Was hat der Sparkassenleiter gesagt?

einladen, lud . . . ein to invite, invited
als Belohnung as a reward
geben, gab + dative to give, gave to someone
bekommen, bekam to get, got

Frame 1: Welcher Tag war es, und welche Jahreszeit?
Wann packte die Familie Schmidt alles ins Auto?
Wie war das Wetter?
War die Familie glücklich? Warum?

die Ferien   holidays
früh am Morgen   early in the morning
in Urlaub fahren   to go on holiday

Frame 2: Wohin fuhr die Familie? Wie war das Wetter?
Freute sich die Familie auf ihren Urlaub?

in den Gebirgen   in the mountains
schneien, schnie   to snow
sich freuen auf + accusative   to look forward to

Frame 3: Wie lange war die Familie unterwegs gewesen, als sie am
Zoll ankam? Was mußte man da dem Beamten zeigen?
Was sagte der Beamte?
In welches Land fuhr die Familie dann?

an der Grenze   at the border
am Zoll   at the customs
der Reisepaß   passport
die Schweiz   Switzerland

Frame 4: Was war los mit dem Auto?
Was sagte Herr Schmidt?
Konnte er das Auto reparieren?

eine Panne haben   to break down
versuchen   to try

Frame 5: Was mußte die Familie machen? Wie war das Wetter?
Wie spät war es? Waren sie glücklich?

zu Fuß gehen   to go on foot
ein Haus suchen   to look for a house
sich Sorgen machen   to be worried

Frame 6: Wie lange war die Familie gelaufen, bevor sie ein
Haus fand? Wer wohnte da?
Was sagten der Bauer und seine Frau?
Was machte die Familie?

'Willkommen!'   'welcome!'

Kaffee trinken   to drink coffee
beim Bauer   at the farmer's house
übernachten   to stay the night

In den Ferien

Frame 1: Wie hieß das Mädchen?
Wo verbrachte es die letzten Sommerferien und mit wem?
Was machte die Familie jeden Tag?

verbringen to spend
die Eltern parents
der Strand beach

Frame 2: Was machte die Familie am Strand?
War das Mädchen zufrieden?

sich sonnen to sunbathe
stricken to knit
lesen to read
sich langweilen to be bored

Frame 3: Was machte das Mädchen?
Was machten ihre Eltern?

allein alone
schwimmen to swim
im Meer in the sea

Frame 4: Was schrie das Mädchen plötzlich?
Was machten ihre Eltern?
Wer lief ins Meer, um dem Mädchen zu helfen?

'Zur Hilfe!' 'help!'
bemerken to notice
der Junge boy
retten to save
helfen + dative to help

Frame 5: Wie ging es dem Mädchen nun?
Wie hieß der Junge?
Was kaufte er?
Gefiel er dem Mädchen?

ein Eis an ice cream
gefallen (+ dative) to please

Frame 6: Was sagte das Mädchen ihren Eltern?
Waren sie glücklich?
Wie ging das Urlaub weiter?

vorstellen to introduce
überrascht surprised
zusammen together
ausgehen to go out

Dienstag

Vocabulary

winken zu (+ dative)   to wave to
das Baby   baby
schreien   to scream
spülen   to wash up
gestreßt   stressed
saubermachen   to clean
der Mantel   coat
die Einkaufstasche   shopping bag
einkaufen gehen   to go shopping
der Supermarkt   supermarket
der Einkaufswagen   shopping trolley
greifen nach (+ dative)   to reach for
die Dose   tin
aussuchen   to look out/choose
nehmen   to take
hinfallen   to fall down
lachen   to laugh
sich ärgern   to be angry
an der Kasse   at the cash desk
grinsen   to grin
einschlafen   to fall asleep
zufrieden   content

Der Unfall

Vocabulary

Weihnachten   Christmas
die Kneipe   bar
die Kollegen   colleagues
in der Ecke   in the corner
der Weihnachtsbaum   Christmas tree
besoffen   drunk
mit dem Taxi   by taxi
sein eigenes Auto   his own car
fahren   to drive
nach Hause   home
frieren   to freeze
schleudern   to skid
an einer Kurve   on a curve
der Notarzt   emergency doctor
tragen   to carry
aufwachen   to wake up
das Krankenhaus   hospital
das Bein   leg
gebrochen   broken
der Verband   bandage

Die Geburtstagsparty

Vocabulary

Geburtstag haben   to have a birthday
enttäuscht   disappointed
vergessen   to forget
die Universität   university
die Vorlesung   lecture
flüstern   to whisper
es klingelt   the doorbell rings
überrascht   surprised
mitbringen   to bring with you
die Flasche Bier/Wein   bottle of beer/wine
die Chips   crisps
die Knabbersachen   savoury snacks
tanzen   to dance
sich amüsieren   to enjoy oneself
'Herzlichen Glückwunsch!'   'Happy Birthday!'
das Geschenk   present

Die erste Verabredung

Vocabulary

die Deutschstunde   German lesson
träumen   to dream
mögen   to like
während der Pause   at break
ausgehen   to go out
heute abend   this evening
schüchtern   shy
sich anziehen   to get dressed
sich freuen auf + accusative   to look forward to
treffen   to meet
voll   full
enttäuscht   disappointed
verlegen   embarrassed
das Café   cafe
sich unterhalten   to converse
spazieren gehen   to go for a walk
Hände halten   to hold hands

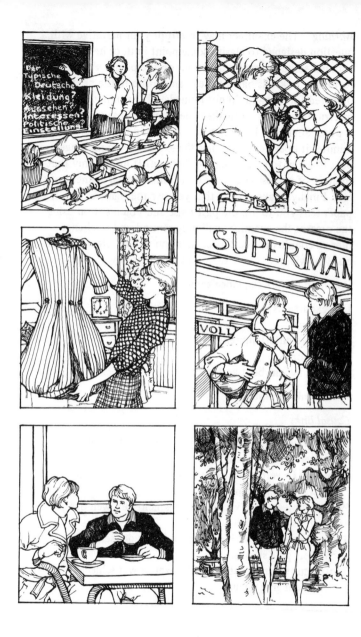

Warning The examiner may interrupt your narrative with a question designed to clarify some point in it, or he may, at the end, use some follow-up questions on the pictures to test you further or link this part of the examination to the next. Be prepared for this and do not immediately assume that he is interrupting or asking further questions because your standard is poor. Similarly, if you are cut off in mid flow after a few minutes it does not mean that the examiner can no longer bear to listen to your appalling German! It means only that there is, of necessity, a strict time limit on each element of the test. Finally, make certain that you use the right tense — if the paper tells you to use the past tense and you insist on using the present the examiner will only remind you to change tense a couple of times: after that you will be allowed to go on but you will be losing vital marks unnecessarily.

Common picture sequence topics

Day excursions — to the country, seaside, etc.
Hotel stays
Parties and entertainments
School stories
Travel — by car, boat and train

Frame-linking phrases

Causal links

Wegen (+ genitive + verb + subject): Wegen des schlechten Wetters ging sie nicht aus.
Deswegen (+ verb + subject): Das Wetter war schlecht, deswegen ging sie nicht aus.
Weil (+ subject . . . + verb): Sie ging nicht aus, weil das Wetter schlecht war.
Trotz (+ genitive + verb + subject): Trotz des schlechten Wetters ging sie aus.
Trotzdem (+ verb + subject): Das Wetter war schlecht, trotzdem ging sie aus.

Temporal links

Nachdem (+ subject . . . + verb): Nachdem sie den Kaffee getrunken hatte, ging sie ins Bett.
Am folgenden Tag (+ verb + subject): Am folgenden Tag ging sie aus.
Am gleichen Tag (+ verb + subject): Am gleichen Tag ging sie aus.
Gleich darauf (+ verb + subject): Gleich darauf ging sie aus.
Kurz darauf (+ verb + subject): Kurz darauf ging sie aus.
Einige Minuten/eine Stunde später (+ verb + subject): Eine Stunde später ging sie aus.

5 The data sheet

This is a new variation on the picture sequence which appears in some examinations, testing your reading comprehension and ability to manipulate German as well as how well you can narrate, usually in the past tense.

Preparation hints

Some boards use this simply as a stimulus for narration like the picture sequence, others use it as a basis for questions which may well involve the future as well as past tense. Obviously, then, your first preparation task is to revise these tenses carefully. As this is an oral exercise you will need the perfect rather than imperfect or simple past. In some ways this is an easier test than being asked to narrate from a series of pictures because you are inevitably given a fair amount of vocabulary, but it does test your ability to manipulate this vocabulary — turning infinitives of verbs into past or future tenses, for example — and to do really well you will need to add something of your own to the information on the sheet.

Read through the sheet carefully, ascertaining whether it is a diary, shopping list, reminder list, timetable etc. and then, if you are to create a narrative from it, prepare in much the same way as you would for the picture sequence. Make up a couple of sentences for each element and then go through it again, linking the parts sensibly. See also if there is anything you can add. For example, if you have the diary entry 'Montag nachmittag — Hallenbad mit Inge'. give the time you went, how, whether you dived, whether it was fun etc. This will impress far more than the bald statement: 'Am Montag Nachmittag bin ich mit Inge zum Hallenbad gegangen', which adds nothing to what is given and only proves that you can cope with the past of 'gehen' and know that 'Hallenbad' is either masculine or neuter. Even the fairly simple 'Am Montag nachmittag sind Inge und ich im Hallenbad schwimmen gegangen,' is an improvement. At least you have shown that you know what a 'Hallenbad' is! Do not, however, be over-ambitious and get more complicated than you are really able in German.

If you are taking an examination in which the data sheet is used as a stimulus for questions study it carefully, thinking of, and answering, as many questions about it as you can. To take the same diary entry as above: you could be asked, 'Was haben Sie am Montag gemacht?', 'Wann sind Sie schwimmen gegangen?', 'Sind Sie alleine zum Schwimmbad gegangen?', 'Sind Sie am Montag einkaufen gegangen?' and so on.

Once in the examination room, listen attentively to the questions so that you give suitable answers. The sheet may be taken as having been written by you, or it may be Frau Wagner's, in which case it is no good answering with 'Ich . . . .' unless, of course, your name is Frau Wagner!

MODEL DATA SHEETS

Mein Tagebuch

Montag: 11 Uhr — Friseur; Nachmittag — Kaffee u. Kuchen bei Schmidt.
Dienstag: putzen; Bücherei.
Mittwoch: an Oma schreiben; Abend — Restaurant Johannsen mit Peter.
Donnerstag: einkaufen, Hose, Bluse; Nachmittag — Wäscherei.
Freitag: Abend — tanzen mit Jörg.
Samstag: 10 Uhr — Reitstunde; Nachmittag — packen.
Sonntag: Urlaub! Schweiz mit Klaus.

Possible questions

1 Beschreiben Sie, was Sie am Montag gemacht haben.
2 Wann haben Sie die Hausarbeit gemacht?
3 Wo sind Sie am Dienstag nachmittag hingegangen, und was haben Sie da gemacht?
4 Mit wem sind Sie essen gegangen, und was haben Sie gegessen?
5 Wo sind Sie einkaufen gegangen?
6 Was haben Sie am Donnerstag nachmittag gemacht?
7 Wo sind Sie am Freitag hingegangen?
8 Sind Sie am Samstag ausgegangen?
9 Was haben Sie gepackt?

10 Was haben Sie am Sonntag gemacht? Wie sind Sie gefahren?

MODEL NARRATIVE

Montag früh ist Jutta zum Friseur gegangen, weil sie am Nachmittag zu Kaffee und Kuchen bei Schmidt eingeladen war. Da hat sie viel geplaudert. Am nächsten Morgen hat sie die Hausarbeit gemacht; sie hat staubgesaugt und alles im Haus aufgeräumt. Danach war sie ziemlich müde, also ist sie zur Bücherei gegangen und hat sich ein Buch ausgesucht. Sie hat eine Detektivgeschichte ausgewählt und mit nach Hause genommen. Am Mittwoch hat Jutta an ihre Oma in Hamburg einen langen Brief geschrieben, und dann hat sie sich ein wenig ausgeruht, weil sie am Abend mit Peter im Restaurant Johannsen gegessen hat. Sie haben ein schönes Essen gehabt, das sehr teuer war, und Jutta ist erst sehr spät ins Bett gegangen. Trotzdem mußte sie am nächsten Morgen früh aufstehen, um in die Stadt zu fahren, wo sie sich eine Hose und eine passende Bluse gekauft hat. Später ist sie mit ihrer schmutzigen Wäsche zur Wäscherei gegangen. Am Freitag abend ist Jutta mit Jörg in eine Diskothek gefahren, und sie haben viel getanzt. Obwohl sie sehr müde war, hat sie am nächsten Morgen bei der Reitschule eine Reitstunde gehabt. Sie ist einmal vom Pferd gefallen. Sie hat den ganzen Nachmittag zu Hause verbracht und alles für ihren Urlaub mit Klaus in der Schweiz in einen Koffer gepackt. Sie ist früh am nächsten Morgen mit Klaus losgefahren.

Nicht vergessen!

Tante Waltraut schreiben
Oma anrufen
Hochzeitseinladungskarten kaufen (50 Stück)
Post – Briefmarken, Paket an Elke
heute – Bank, Metzger, 1430 Zahnarzt
Samstag 1130 Friseur
Samstag Abend – 2000 Uhr, Richard (Essen, Kino)
Dienstag – Party bei Christiane

Possible questions

1 An wen muß Heike diese Woche schreiben?
2 Mit wem wird sie telefonieren?
3 Wann geht sie mit Richard aus?
4 Was hat sie heute nachmittag gemacht?

5 Warum geht man zum Metzger?
6 Wann läßt sich Heike die Haare schneiden?
7 Wieviele Gäste werden zur Hochzeit kommen?
8 Wer wird diese Woche eine Party geben?
9 Was hat Heike an der Post gemacht?
10 Sie sind Heike, und es ist Sonntag: erzählen Sie, was Sie gestern gemacht haben!

MODEL NARRATIVE

Heike hat diese Woche viel zu tun. Vorgestern hat sie einen langen Brief an ihre Tante Waltraut geschrieben, die zur Zeit im Krankenhaus liegt. Sie hat auch ihre Oma angerufen, um ihr zu erzählen, wie es geht und was sie neulich gemacht hat. Gestern ist Heike in die Stadt gefahren, wo sie 50 Hochzeitseinladungskarten gekauft hat. Sie heiratet nämlich in zwei Monaten. Sie hat auch Briefmarken für die Karten gekauft und ein Paket für ihre Freundin Elke an der Post abgegeben. Heute muß Heike wieder in die Stadt fahren, um beim Metzger Fleisch zu kaufen. Vorher geht sie zur Bank und holt sich etwas Geld. Heute nachmittag um halb drei geht sie zum Zahnarzt, weil sie Zahnschmerzen hat. Um halb elf am Samstag wird Heike sich die Haare beim Friseur schneiden lassen, also wird sie am Abend sehr schön aussehen, wenn sie mit ihrem Verlobten Richard ins Restaurant und danach ins Kino geht. Sie werden einen neuen Film aus Frankreich sehen. Nächsten Dienstag gibt eine Freundin von Heike, Christiane, eine Party. Heike wird mit Richard dahingehen.

Letzten Dienstag

0730 aufgestanden, Bett machen, Hausarbeit
0900 Stadt – Lebensmittelgeschäft, Stadtbücherei, Metzger.
        – Mittagessen beim griechischen Restaurant
           mit Karin.
        – Bus nach Hause (viel zu tragen!)
1500 Geigenunterricht – schwierig!
1700 Haare waschen; alles umgeräumt für Party
2000 Gäste. 25 Leute: tanzen im Wohnzimmer; Wein, Bier, Cola. kaltes Büffet in der Küche. Viel Spaß!
zwei Uhr morgens ins Bett – geschafft!

Try your own narrative to this one.

6   The prepared topic

Many CSE and GCE boards include a conversation based on a prepared topic in their oral examination. The fact that you have been allowed to prepare the subject matter of this part of your conversation gives you a chance really to show off your fluency and accuracy in the language without having to search your mind for specialist vocabulary. Although your topic may be on some aspect of Germany or German culture, you are not being tested on factual knowledge but on your use of the language.

Preparation hints

Some boards provide you with a list of topics from which you must choose between one and four, others leave the choice of topic entirely up to you, in which case you will find the list at the end of this chapter useful. Once you have chosen your subject you are left with the vague instruction to 'prepare' it. You will find this a great deal easier if you have chosen a subject about which you know something so that you have some firm facts to go on. Try to imagine the sort of questions an examiner, or indeed any intersted person, would ask on this topic. For example, if you have chosen 'Sport in Deutschland' you will probably be asked what sports are popular in Germany, what the 'Bundesliga' is, where in Germany you can ski, where sail, maybe even if you can name some famous German sportsmen and women etc. Think of specialist words you would need to talk about sport — match, race, stadium, local derby, umpire, referee etc. — and make sure you look them up and learn them. You will not be expected to explain the rules of a game in detail — even an English person cannot always explain the rules of cricket clearly — but you will definitely need specialist vocabulary.

You may find that you can think most clearly in your preparation if you write out a short talk in full. This must

not, however, be learnt by heart and spouted at the long-suffering examiner. All the syllabuses stress that a topic is to be prepared as a basis for conversation or discussion, not as a lecture. If, in the examination room, you do start to lecture you will find yourself interrupted very quickly by questions. If you have fixed a lecture in your mind and ignore or allow yourself to be flustered by questions you will find yourself in trouble. This is a test of your German, not of your capacity for learning by heart, and the preparation time is to help you sort out your ideas and look up specialised vocabulary.

Some boards allow you to take things into the room to talk about. This is an excellent idea as it gives you a very solid base for conversation. For example, if you want to talk about a German town you know or a stay in Germany take in any photographs or postcards you have. It is much easier to describe something if you have a picture in front of you, and it gives you and your examiner something more interesting to look at than each other!

Finally, if you are taking the examination for a board which limits preparation time to a few minutes just before the test use the following list to anticipate and prepare vocabulary needs. The themes do not vary greatly.

Possible topics

Choose your topics carefully: some may look easy until you consider what you might be asked on such a theme! 'Deutsch' or 'Deutschland' can be taken to mean any German-speaking country so you can use Austria and Switzerland as well as Germany itself.

Food

Essen und Trinken (in Deutschland)

Free time

Sport in Deutschland
Die Sommerferien
Meine Hobbys

The future

Meine Pläne für die Zukunft

German culture

Sport in Deutschland
Weihnachten in Deutschland
Ein berühmter Deutscher/eine berühmte Deutsche
Essen und Trinken in Deutschland
Ein deutsches Buch/ein deutscher Film, das/der mir gut
gefallen hat
Deutsches Fernsehen und/oder Radio

Germany

Ein Fluß in Deutschland
Eine Stadt/ein Dorf in Deutschland
Das deutsche Verkehrswesen
Das deutsche Schulsystem

Media

Deutsche Zeitungen und Zeitschriften
Ein deutsches Buch/ein deutscher Film, das/der mir gut gefallen
hat
Deutsches Fernsehen und/oder Radio

School

Das deutsche Schulsystem
Das Leben in der Schule

Shopping

In der Stadt
Auf dem Postamt

Sport

Sport in Deutschland
Sport
Meine Hobbys

Travel

Eine Reise nach Deutschland
das deutsche Verkehrswesen
Reisen
Die Sommerferien

7 The prepared questions

This is a slight variation on the General Conversation which some CSE and GCE boards use. Lists of between fifty and eighty questions of varying difficulty are circulated to schools at least a term before the examination for candidates to prepare. Like the prepared topic, this is a test of your fluency and grammatical accuracy. The examiner will ask you between ten and twenty of these, some easy and some requiring more complicated answers: since you have had time to prepare, there should be no comprehension difficulties, and he will be looking for prompt, idiomatic and grammatically correct responses.

Preparation hints

Work through the question list carefully and methodically, looking up and learning unknown vocabulary. You will not have the list in front of you in the examination, so make sure you know how new words sound, not just how they look. Make up and note down a concise answer to each question, thinking about the grammar as you do so. Say the answers to yourself a few times before you write them down — they are to sound natural like spoken German, not literary German which you learn and recite. Learn your answers, but try to avoid the trap of rigid learning without understanding what you are saying. If your pre-learned answers desert you in the examination room because you are nervous it will do no good to sit silent and panic! You must have enough general understanding, gained during careful preparation of the questions, to produce some sort of sensible answer.

Sample questions

You will be asked a fairly even mixture of straightforward and more complicated ones.

Straightforward questions

1. Wie groß ist Ihre Familie?
2. Wie können Sie im Haushalt helfen?
3. Was ziehen Sie für die Schule an?
4. Wie lange dauert eine Unterrichtsstunde in dieser Schule?
5. Wieviele Schüler gibt es in Ihrer Deutschklasse?
6. Wie alt sind Sie am letzten Geburtstag geworden?
7. Was werden Sie tun, wenn Sie die Schule verlassen?
8. Welche Verkehrsmittel gibt es in Ihrer Stadt/Ihrem Dorf?
9. Wo gehen Sie hin, wenn Sie Brot kaufen wollen?
10. Sie wollen Obst kaufen — was sagen Sie zum Händler?
11. Wie geben Sie Ihr Taschengeld aus?
12. Sie wollen nach Deutschland fahren — wie können Sie fahren?
13. Wo waren Sie letztes Jahr im Urlaub?
14. Wohin werden Sie dieses Jahr fahren?
15. Wann braucht man einen Reisepaß?
16. Welche Frage stellt Ihnen an der Grenze der Zollbeamte?
17. Wo kann man am billigsten übernachten, wenn man auf Reisen ist?
18. Wann sind Sie das letzte Mal ins Ausland gereist?
19. Wann fängt die Schule gewöhnlich morgens in Deutschland an?
20. Seit wie lange lernen Sie schon Deutsch?
21. Wann waren Sie das letzte Mal im Kino?
22. Wie sind Sie heute zur Schule gekommen?
23. Was machen Sie nächstes Wochenende?
24. Wie groß ist der Ort, in dem Sie wohnen?
25. Wann braucht man einen Führerschein?

More complicated questions

1. Welche deutsche Stadt würden Sie gern besuchen und warum?
2. Beschreiben Sie eine typische deutsche Mahlzeit!
3. Welche Unterschiede gibt es zwischen einer deutschen und einer englischen Schule?
4. Beschreiben Sie Ihren Vater/Bruder/Ihre Mutter/Schwester!
5. Welchen Tag der Woche haben Sie am liebsten und warum?
6. Beschreiben Sie Ihr Haus!
7. Beschreiben Sie ein interessantes Gebäude in dieser Gegend!

8   Was möchten Sie später werden und warum?

9   Möchten Sie lieber auf dem Lande oder in der Stadt wohnen und warum?

10 Was sind die Vor- und Nachteile des Lebens auf dem Lande/in der Stadt?

11 Was sind die Vor- und Nachteile einer Gesamtschule?

12 Wo möchten Sie am liebsten Ihr Urlaub verbringen und warum?

13 Was sind die Vor- und Nachteile eines Campingurlaubs?

14 Wie könnte man in der Freizeit Geld verdienen?

15 Sie wollen eine Schallplatte kaufen: erzählen Sie, was Sie im Geschäft tun!

16 Was ist ein 'Ausverkauf'?

17 Was würden Sie tun, wenn Sie sehr reich wären?

18 Was ist eine Einbahnstraße?

19 Was ist eine Fußgängerzone?

20 Was ist der Unterschied zwischen einem D-Zug und einem Personenzug?

21 Sie wollen in Deutschland einen Reisescheck einlösen: wohin gehen Sie, und was machen Sie da?

22 Welches fremde Land möchten Sie am liebsten besuchen und warum?

23 Möchten Sie in Deutschland wohnen? Warum/warum nicht?

24 Warum ist das 'Abitur' für einen Schüler so wichtig?

25 Was bedeutet 'sitzenbleiben' in einer deutschen Schule?

8 The reading passage

This test is found in various forms in both CSE and 'O' level examinations. On the whole, CSE boards ask you to read aloud either a selection of sentences or a short paragraph, whilst 'O' level boards set a longer narrative passage of about two paragraphs. This element of the oral test is above all a test of your pronunciation and intonation and also, indirectly, of your comprehension, since you can only read really well if you understand what you are reading.

Preparation hints

Reading aloud well is not easy in any language, so practice is necessary. Take any chances there are to read aloud in class, whatever the lesson: none of this experience goes to waste. As the examination approaches, concentrate on reading German aloud — in class, or just to yourself — on breathing in the right places for the sense, on getting your tongue round long compound words and on making questions sound like questions (by raising tone at the end). Certain things are particularly noticed in this test, above all, your pronunciation of vowels, with and without the Umlaut. Practise on these pairs of words, and notice how vital an Umlaut can be in utterly changing the meaning of a word:

> schon   schön
> Hut   Hüte
> Stadt   Städte

Make sure also that you have the pronunciation of diphthongs — pairs of vowels — clear in your mind:

> B*ein*   — 'eye'
> B*ie*ne — 'ee'
> B*au*m   — 'ow'
> B*äu*me — 'oy'
> L*eu*te — 'oy'

In the time you are given to prepare the actual examination passage, read it through first to understand the gist of what it is about. Unless you know what you are saying you will not read well. Read the passage through again, more slowly, if possible aloud, deciding where to breathe. If there is direct speech involved, put some expression into it. Once you are in the examination room, do not let your nerves push you into reading so fast that you stumble over every second word. On the other hand, do not read so slowly that each word is isolated and no meaning is conveyed. Read carefully and clearly, putting across the meaning as well as your perfect German accent. Put as much expression into your reading as you can.

Sample reading tests

Use the following passages and sentences for practice. Take particular care over the words printed in italics — these are the ones which can cause pronunciation problems. The part of the word which is underlined is the part on which to put the stress each time and possible breathing spaces are marked by a diagonal line.

Sentences

1 Der V*a*ter *stopfte* sei*ne Pfeife.*
2 Ich g*e*he in die *Drogerie* und die *Bäckerei.*
3 Da ist ein *Segelboot* auf der *See.*
4 Im *Herbst* wird das Wetter *kälter.*
5 Karl fährt in den *Sommerferien* nach *England.*
6 Ich *möchte* ein Zimmer für eine *Person.*
7 Die M*u*tter *kniete* sich hin und *scheuerte* den Fußboden.
8 Sie haben zwei *Söhne* und eine *Tochter.*
9 Das *Orchester* spielt im *Konzert.*
10 *Bayern-*München spielt gegen Eintracht *Frankfurt.*

(ALSEB, CSE)

DIALOGUES

Passage 1

1 You are allowed five minutes to study the passage below and will retain the passage during the remainder of the test.

2 The examiner will read aloud the title and the part of the 'Kassiererin'. You must read the part of **Andrea.**

3 After you have read the passage you will have an informal general conversation with the examiner.

Kassiererin: Guten Tag, kann ich euch helfen?

Andrea: Guten Tag, /ich möchte gerne zwei *Schülerkarten* / für mich und meine Freundin.

Kassiererin: Habt ihr denn auch eure Schülerausweise bei euch?

Andrea: Ich glaube ja. Ich werde mal *nachsehen.* Der meine muß irgendwo hier sein.

Kassiererin: Dann zeig ihn mir bitte, ich darf dir sonst nämlich keine Schülerkarte geben.

Andrea: Oh *verflixt,* /ich habe meinen *Ausweis vergessen.* Er ist in meiner *Anoraktasche,* /und heute/habe ich meinen *Mantel* an.

Kassiererin: Hat deine Freundin denn ihren Ausweis?

Andrea: Ja,/sie hat ihn in der *Hand.*

Kassiererin: Na, dann will ich heute mal ein Auge zudrücken und dir auch eine Schülerkarte geben.

Andrea: Oh, vielen Dank, /das ist sehr nett von Ihnen. Können Sie uns bitte sagen, /wo die Kabinen sind, /wo wir uns *umziehen* können?

(NWREB, CSE)

Passage 2

1 You are allowed five minutes to study the passage below and will retain the passage during the remainder of the test.

2 The examiner will read aloud the title and the part of **Bernd.** You must read the part of **Stefan.**

3 After you have read the passage you will have an informal general conversation with the examiner.

Bernd: Stefan, hast du Lust, mit mir auf den Jahrmarkt zu gehen?

Stefan: Wie ist der *Jahrmarkt*?

Bernd: Es ist ein großer Jahrmarkt. Sie haben ein Riesenrad und eine ganze Menge Buden.

Stefan: Prima,/ ich komme mit dir. Ich möchte gerne / an einer *Schießbude* mein *Glück* versuchen,/und ich glaube,/

ich habe noch *genug* Geld,/um mir dann/eine *Bratwurst* zu kaufen. Komm,/steig auf dein *Fahrrad,* / laß uns hinfahren.

Bernd: Guck mal, Stefan, dahinten ist das Riesenrad. Es ist wirklich riesig, nicht wahr?

Stefan: Ja,/ich glaube aber,/daß ich darauf/nicht fahren werde. Mir wird ja *schon* beim *Zuschauen schlecht.* Was *hältst* du davon,/wenn wir uns hier/in einer halben Stunde/ wiedertreffen. Dann kann jeder das tun,/was er möchte.

(NWREB, CSE)

Passage 3

Herr Krämer hatte einen *anstrengenden* Tag im *Büro* gehabt/ und *achtete* nicht auf das *Tachometer,* / *während* er durch die Stadt/nach Hause fuhr. *Plötzlich* / erblickte er im *Rückspiegel* einen Polizeiwagen,/der ihn bald *überholte* /und ein *Signal* gab, /daß er halten sollte. 'Den *Führerschein,* / bitte,/ 'sagte der *Polizist.* 'Wissen Sie,/ wie schnell Sie gefahren sind?' 'Leider/ habe ich keine Ahnung,' /*antwortete* Herr Krämer. '100 *Stundenkilometer*,' sagte der *Polizist.*

(ALSEB, CSE)

Passage 4

Samstagmorgen /standen wir immer *früh* auf. Heute/*regnete* es *stark*; wir zogen/*also*/unsere *Regenmäntel* an/und gingen zur *Garage.* Vater *schloß* auf/und fuhr den Wagen *rückwärts* auf die Straße. Wir *stiegen* schnell ein/und fuhren *los.* Nach *zwanzig* Minuten/*erreichten* wir den großen Parkplatz in der *Stadtmitte.* Vater warf eine *Münze* in die *Parkuhr:* /es kostete zehn *Pfennig* für eine halbe Stunde.

(YREB, CSE)

Passage 5

Karl *saß* nachmittags mit zwei Fremden im *Wirtshaus* /und spielte Karten. Nach einiger Zeit / kam ein Freund zu ihnen ins *Lokal* /und *bemerkte,* / daß die beiden Fremden sich unter den Tisch *beugten* /und dabei Karten *austauschten.* Er rief Karl nach draußen/und machte ihn auf den Betrug aufmerksam. Zu seiner *Überraschung/empörte* Karl sich *überhaupt* nicht,/blieb sehr gelassen,/sogar *still vergnügt*/und sagte *schließlich:*/'Ach, weißt du,/es ist nicht so schlimm,/wenn sie sich *bücken*/und Karten *austauschen.* Das habe ich *längst* gemerkt. Aber/wenn sie unter dem Tisch verschwinden,/nehme ich ihnen oben das Geld weg,/das *gleicht* sich aus.'

(Cambridge, GCE)

Passage 6

Paul Berger redete sehr wenig,/verlangte/aber/von den Leuten,/ die bei ihm *arbeiteten,*/daß sie seine *Befehle* sofort *befolgten.* Da er nun meinte,/daß beim *Sprechen* zu viel Zeit verloren ging,/ befahl er/am liebsten/durch *Zeichen.* Eines Tages/stellte er einen neuen *Knecht* ein/und sagte zu ihm:

'Hör mal,/ich mach nicht viele Worte./Also/wenn ich dir mit dem *Finger* winke,/dann kommst du.'

Der *Knecht* dachte einen Augenblick *darüber* nach/und sagte dann:/'Ich glaube,/Herr Berger,/daß wir uns gut verstehen werden,/denn ich mache auch nicht viele Worte. Wenn ich also den Kopf *schüttle,*/dann komm ich nicht.'

(Cambridge, GCE)